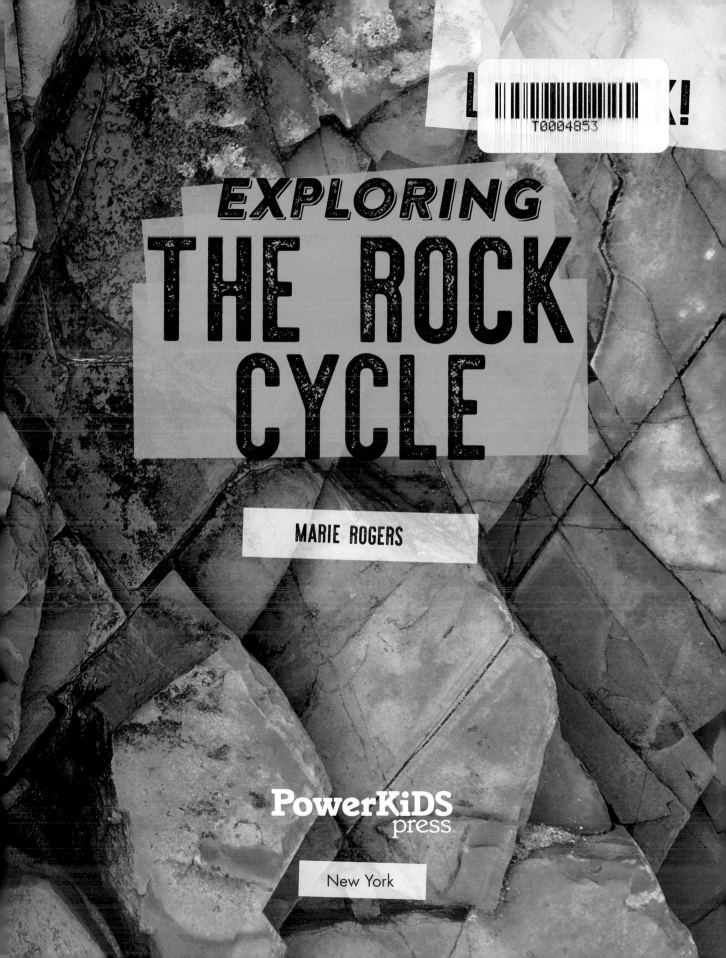

EXPLORING
THE ROCK CYCLE

MARIE ROGERS

PowerKiDS press

New York

Published in 2022 by The Rosen Publishing Group, Inc.
29 East 21st Street, New York, NY 10010

First Edition

Portions of this work were originally authored by Maria Nelson and published as *The Rock Cycle*. All new material in this edition authored by Marie Rogers.

Editor: Amanda Vink
Cover Designer: Alan Sliwinski
Interior Designer: Rachel Rising

Photo Credits: Cover 3rn4/Shutterstock.com; Cover, pp. 1, 3, 4, 5, 6, 7, 8, 9, 10, 12, 13, 14,1 6,18, 20, 21, 22, 23, 24 (background) Alex Konon/Shutterstock.com; p. 5 Nasky/Shutterstock.com; p. 6 Naeblys/Shutterstock.com; p. 7 shooarts/Shutterstock.com; p. 8 cameilia/Shutterstock.com; p. 9 yavuz sariyildiz/ Moment/Getty Images; p. 10 Fedorov Oleksiy/Shutterstock.com; p. 11 Fez Fez/500px/Getty Images; p. 13 presented by Zolashine/Moment/Getty Images; p. 15 Microgen/Shutterstock.com; p. 16 vvoe/Shutterstock.com; p. 17 LesPalenik/Shutterstock.com; p. 18 Ralf Lehmann/Shutterstock.com; p. 19 Marius Roman/Moment/Getty Images; p. 20 Martina Badini/Shutterstock.com; p. 21 Jeffrey B. Banke/ Shutterstock.com; p. 22 anaken2012/Shutterstock.com.

Some of the images in this book illustrate individuals who are models. The depictions do not imply actual situations or events.

Cataloging-in-Publication Data

Names: Rogers, Marie.
Title: Exploring the rock cycle / Marie Rogers.
Description: New York : PowerKids Press, 2022. | Series: Let's rock! | Includes glossary and index.
Identifiers: ISBN 9781725319295 (pbk.) | ISBN 9781725319318 (library bound) | ISBN 9781725319301 (6 pack)
Subjects: LCSH: Petrology–Juvenile literature. | Geochemical cycles–Juvenile literature.
Classification: LCC QE432.2 R5936 2022 | DDC 552–dc23

Manufactured in the United States of America

CPSIA Compliance Information: Batch #CWPK22. For further information contact Rosen Publishing, New York, New York at 1-800-237-9932.

Find us on

CONTENTS

OUR EARTH 4

LAYERS 6

THE ROCK CYCLE 8

WEATHERING AWAY 10

EROSION 12

SEDIMENTARY ROCK 14

METAMORPHIC ROCK 16

IGNEOUS ROCK 18

UPLIFT 20

DISCOVERING EARTH'S HISTORY 22

GLOSSARY 23

INDEX 24

WEBSITES 24

OUR EARTH

People have long wondered how Earth formed, how long it's been here, and what makes it up. Luckily, clues are all around us—in rocks!

In the 18th century, scientist John Hutton had an idea. He said the rocks that make up Earth have been slowly forming, breaking down, and reforming in the same way for a long time—since Earth formed 4.5 billion years ago. This is called the rock cycle. Rocks will continue to move through the rock cycle as long as the conditions of the planet remain the same. Knowing about the rock cycle has allowed us to uncover Earth's history.

The rock cycle helps us understand the conditions that formed different rocks. That tells us about the state of the planet at different times through history.

ROCKING OUT

Movements in the rock cycle take a long time—often millions of years. During the cycle of a human life, it seems like most rocks are **permanent**, but that's because we're not usually around long enough.

THE ROCK CYCLE

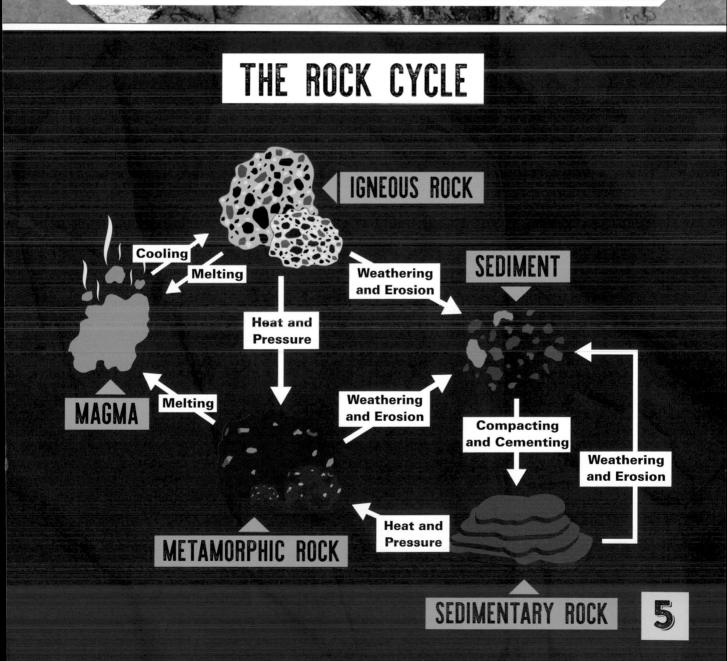

IGNEOUS ROCK

Cooling

Melting

Weathering and Erosion

SEDIMENT

Heat and Pressure

MAGMA

Melting

Weathering and Erosion

Compacting and Cementing

Weathering and Erosion

METAMORPHIC ROCK

Heat and Pressure

SEDIMENTARY ROCK

LAYERS

Earth has three main layers. At the center is Earth's core, located around 1,802 miles (2,900 km) below the surface. It's **dense**, very hot, and made mostly of iron and nickel. Earth's middle layer is the mantle. It's mostly solid rock and makes up 84 percent of Earth's total volume. Where **temperatures** are hotter, it's liquid. Activity in the mantle helps create the landforms on Earth's crust. This hard, outer shell is where humans live.

Together, the crust and upper part of the mantle are the lithosphere. This layer is divided into pieces of moving rock called tectonic plates. They slide past one another and run into each other.

TECTONIC PLATES

ROCKING OUT

Earth has nine major tectonic plates and many smaller ones. The heat from Earth's mantle—like water boiling on a stove—causes them to move. This movement creates mountains, seas, and volcanoes.

Earth's crust is very thin—only 1 percent of the planet's mass!

CRUST

MANTLE

CORE

THE ROCK CYCLE

The lithosphere is where the rock cycle occurs. The rock here can be one of three different kinds. Rocks can move elsewhere in the rock cycle when they are exposed to certain changes in their **environment**.

Earth's crust is made mostly of sedimentary rock, which forms when tiny bits of sand, clay, or pebbles—called sediment—press together and become solid. Metamorphic rock forms from existing rock that changes because of forces in its environment, such as heat or pressure. Igneous rock forms when hot, melted rock from within Earth cools.

PEBBLES ▶

8

ROCKING OUT

Rocks are nonliving solids made of **minerals**, and different types of rocks have different types of minerals. But a rock's **chemical** makeup is only one part of it. How a rock forms makes a big difference in how it looks!

SAND

Sediment can include different-sized materials, including **boulders**, gravel, sand, and silt.

WEATHERING AWAY

Weathering is when rocks break down into small pieces. Weathering can cause rock to move in the rock cycle.

Weathering can happen when water flows into a rock and freezes. Ice takes up more space and causes the rock to crack. Mixtures of water and minerals can also cause changes to a rock. Tiny living things called bacteria give off chemicals that can make a rock softer and easier to break. This is an example of chemical weathering. Wind blowing over rock for a long time can weather it too. This is an example of physical weathering. Plant growth can also create cracks in rocks.

These granite rock structures in Flinders Chase National Park in Australia were created by weathering.

11

EROSION

When sediment is created and **transported** from its original location, that's called erosion. Wind is a common means of erosion. Gravity, too, can add to erosion. It pulls sediment and loose rock down mountains. Water is a major contributor to erosion. Rain and runoff, or water not taken in by the ground, carries sediment away. The ocean also repeatedly hits the shore and takes sediment with it.

When the energy carrying sediment is used up, the sediment is **deposited** in a new place. Over time, more and more sediment is added to the location, and the layers may start to get very heavy.

Scientists believe water first appeared on Earth about 3.5 billion years ago. Today, water is a very important part of Earth's processes.

ROCKING OUT

Glaciers are huge ice masses that move over land. They're formed when snow and ice pile up and don't melt. Instead, they **compact**. As they move, glaciers rip up rock and may carry it many miles away.

SEDIMENTARY ROCK

When loose sediment piles up, the pressure starts to increase on the lower layers. That rock compacts and takes up less space. This is called the lithification process. Water mixtures flow into open spaces and leave behind minerals that bind the sediment together. This creates sedimentary rock! Chemical precipitation also creates sedimentary rock. That's what happens when a lake dries up over many thousands of years. Mineral deposits, rocks, and organic remains are left behind.

Sedimentary rock often holds fossils. These are the leftover traces of animal and plant life from years gone by. These organic remains are buried and slowly turn into rock.

Paleontologists are scientists who study fossils. They discover clues about how animals and plants lived on Earth millions of years ago.

METAMORPHIC ROCK

Some rock stays on the surface for a long time. Other times, rock is forced deeper into Earth. Underground conditions can change a rock. These changes can also occur at tectonic plate boundaries.

Metamorphic rocks begin as one type of rock and turn into another. They're changed by heat, pressure, and sometimes hot mineral liquids. The rock doesn't melt, but it can be twisted and shaped. This can also sometimes change its chemical makeup. These changes can affect any existing type of rock—sedimentary, igneous, and metamorphic rock can all change again!

BANDS OF CRYSTALS

Sometimes metamorphic rocks reform with bands of crystals.

IGNEOUS ROCK

If rock goes too far below the surface, it's subjected to high heat from the mantle. The rock melts into molten rock, which is called magma.

When magma comes to an area that's not as hot, it cools into rock. This is igneous rock. If the rock cools slowly underground, it will have large crystals. This is intrusive igneous rock. If it cools quickly—often because molten rock is forced to the surface, where it becomes lava—then it will have very small crystals or, sometimes, none at all. This is called extrusive igneous rock.

LAVA ▶

Igneous rock often forms the core of mountain ranges.

UPLIFT

When tectonic plates run into each other, sometimes rock is forced to the surface. This process is called uplift. Some scientists believe Earth wouldn't be able to support life without this process. The rock cycle would stop after a time, and Earth's existing mountains and hills would wear away completely. All would be flat.

Uplift can create mountains and hills. It explains why Mount Everest, Earth's highest mountain above sea level, is made of limestone—a sedimentary rock that formed long ago on the ocean floor. Once rocks come to the surface, they're exposed to the forces of weathering and erosion—and the rock cycle continues.

MOUNT EVEREST ▶

ROCKING OUT

Events such as earthquakes cause shifts
in rock. Earthquakes can occur when tectonic plates
run into each other. Thousands of earthquakes
happen every day. About 80 percent occur in
the Ring of Fire in the Pacific Ocean.

Uplift can happen gradually over many years or it can happen
all at once during an event such as an earthquake!

DISCOVERING EARTH'S HISTORY

The rock cycle has no real beginning or end—rocks change into different forms all the time. Even right now, rocks are slowly changing.

Scientists use **radioactive** dating to figure out how long ago rocks formed. The world is full of naturally occurring radioactive elements, and over time these **decay** at a constant rate. Scientists can date fossils and rock layers to create a timeline. Using this information, we've been able to answer many of the questions people have about the planet. The rock cycle will continue, and it will still reveal information about Earth's past!

GLOSSARY

boulder: A very large stone or rounded piece of rock.

chemical: Matter that can be mixed with other matter to cause changes, or having to do with chemicals.

compact: To press something so it fills less space.

decay: To break down.

dense: Having parts that are close together.

deposit: To put something down and leave it behind.

environment: The conditions that surround a thing and affect it.

mineral: A naturally occurring solid substance that is not of plant or animal origin.

permanent: Lasting for a long time or always.

radioactive: Having or producing a powerful form of energy called radiation.

temperature: How hot or cold something is.

transport: To move from one place to another.

INDEX

C
chemical weathering, 10
core (Earth), 6, 7
crust, 6, 7, 8
crystals, 16, 17, 18

E
erosion, 5, 12, 20
extrusive igneous rock, 18

G
glaciers, 13
gravity, 12

I
ice, 10, 13
igneous rock, 5, 8, 16, 18, 19
intrusive igneous rock, 18

L
lava, 18
lithification, 14
lithosphere, 6, 8

M
magma, 5, 18
mantle, 6, 7, 18
metamorphic rock, 5, 8, 16, 17
minerals, 9, 10, 14, 16

P
physical weathering, 10

S
sediment, 5, 8, 9, 12, 14
sedimentary rock, 5, 8, 14, 16, 20

T
tectonic plates, 6, 7, 16, 20, 21

U
uplift, 20, 21

W
water, 10, 12, 14
weathering, 5, 10, 11, 20
wind, 10, 12

WEBSITES

Due to the changing nature of Internet links, PowerKids Press has developed an online list of websites related to the subject of this book. This site is updated regularly. Please use this link to access the list:
www.powerkidslinks.com/letsrock/therockcycle